BASIC SET #1

RUDIMENTS EXAM SERIES

By Glory St. Germain ARCT RMT MYCC UMTC &
Shelagh McKibbon-U'Ren RMT UMTC

ULTIMATE
MUSIC THEORY

GSG MUSIC

Enriching Lives Through Music Education

ISBN: 978-1-927641-02-6

The Ultimate Music Theory™ Program
Enriching Lives Through Music Education

The Ultimate Music Theory™ Workbooks & Answer Books Program includes:

UMT Rudiments Workbooks for Prep 1, Prep 2, Basic, Intermediate, Advanced & Complete
UMT Exam Series (Set #1 & Set #2) for Preparatory, Basic, Intermediate & Advanced

Supplemental Workbooks for PREP LEVEL, LEVELS 1 - 8 & COMPLETE LEVEL
UMT Supplemental Exam Series for LEVEL 5, LEVEL 6, LEVEL 7 & LEVEL 8

The Ultimate Music Theory Program is the *Way to Score Success* as UMT helps students prepare for nationally recognized theory examinations including the Royal Conservatory of Music.

 Library and Archives Canada Cataloguing in Publication. UMT Workbooks & Exam Series /Glory St. Germain & Shelagh McKibbon-U'Ren. Respect Copyright. All rights reserved. GlorylandPublishing.com

Ultimate Music Theory Rudiments Exam Series

GP - EPS1	ISBN: 978-1-927641-00-2	Preparatory Rudiments Exams Set #1
GP - EPS1A	ISBN: 978-1-927641-08-8	Preparatory Exams Answers Set #1
GP - EPS2	ISBN: 978-1-927641-01-9	Preparatory Rudiments Exams Set #2
GP - EPS2A	ISBN: 978-1-927641-09-5	Preparatory Exams Answers Set #2
GP - EBS1	ISBN: 978-1-927641-02-6	Basic Rudiments Exams Set #1
GP - EBS1A	ISBN: 978-1-927641-10-1	Basic Exams Answers Set #1
GP - EBS2	ISBN: 978-1-927641-03-3	Basic Rudiments Exams Set #2
GP - EBS2A	ISBN: 978-1-927641-11-8	Basic Exams Answers Set #2
GP - EIS1	ISBN: 978-1-927641-04-0	Intermediate Rudiments Exams Set #1
GP - EIS1A	ISBN: 978-1-927641-12-5	Intermediate Exams Answers Set #1
GP - EIS2	ISBN: 978-1-927641-05-7	Intermediate Rudiments Exams Set #2
GP - EIS2A	ISBN: 978-1-927641-13-2	Intermediate Exams Answers Set #2
GP - EAS1	ISBN: 978-1-927641-06-4	Advanced Rudiments Exams Set #1
GP - EAS1A	ISBN: 978-1-927641-14-9	Advanced Exams Answers Set #1
GP - EAS2	ISBN: 978-1-927641-07-1	Advanced Rudiments Exams Set #2
GP - EAS2A	ISBN: 978-1-927641-15-6	Advanced Exams Answers Set #2

Ultimate Music Theory Supplemental Exam Series

GP-L5E	ISBN: 978-1-990358-11-1	LEVEL 5 Exams
GP-L5EA	ISBN: 978-1-990358-12-8	LEVEL 5 Exams Answers
GP-L6E	ISBN: 978-1-990358-13-5	LEVEL 6 Exams
GP-L6EA	ISBN: 978-1-990358-14-2	LEVEL 6 Exams Answers
GP-L7E	ISBN: 978-1-990358-15-9	LEVEL 7 Exams
GP-L7EA	ISBN: 978-1-990358-16-6	LEVEL 7 Exams Answers
GP-L8E	ISBN: 978-1-990358-17-3	LEVEL 8 Exams
GP-L8EA	ISBN: 978-1-990358-18-0	LEVEL 8 Exams Answers

Go to UltimateMusicTheory.com and check out the FREE Resources

Ultimate Music Theory FREE RESOURCES created just for you!

The **Ultimate Music Theory Exams** reinforce the **UMT Basic Rudiments Workbook** and prepare students for continued learning with UMT Intermediate Rudiments.

Basic Rudiments Theory Examination requirements are:

Pitch
- Grand Staff (Treble Clef or G Clef and Bass Clef or F Clef)
- Note names (up to five ledger lines below and above the Treble Clef and Bass Clef)
- Accidentals (sharp, flat and natural signs)
- Whole tones (whole steps), diatonic & chromatic semitones (half steps) and enharmonic equivalents

Rhythm
- Note and rest time values (whole, half, quarter, eighth and sixteenth)
- Dotted half notes, dotted quarter notes and dotted eighth notes
- Triplets (quarter notes, eighth notes and sixteenth notes)
- Adding Time Signatures, bar lines and rests to a given line of music (which may include an anacrusis)
- Simple Time Signatures ($\frac{2}{2}$, ¢, $\frac{3}{2}$, $\frac{4}{2}$, $\frac{2}{4}$, $\frac{3}{4}$, $\frac{4}{4}$, C, $\frac{2}{8}$, $\frac{3}{8}$ and $\frac{4}{8}$)

Scales in Major and minor keys up to and including four sharps and four flats
- Major and relative minor (natural, harmonic and melodic) scales, ascending and descending
- Key Signatures (Major and relative minor)
- Tonic, Subdominant and Dominant scale degrees

Triads in Major and harmonic minor keys up to and including four sharps and four flats
- Write or identify: Solid triads (blocked) in Root Position (close position only) beginning on the Tonic, Subdominant and Dominant notes (with or without a Key Signature)
- Identify: Broken triads in Root Position (close position only) beginning on the Tonic, Subdominant and Dominant notes (with or without a Key Signature)

Intervals - Perfect, Major and minor
- Write or identify: above a given note, all intervals up to and including an octave (no inversions), melodic or harmonic form (with or without a Key Signature)
- Identify: below a given note, all intervals up to and including an octave (no inversions), melodic form only (with or without a Key Signature)

Recognition of Key Signatures up to and including four sharps and four flats
- Identify the key (Major or minor) of a given melody with a Key Signature

Transposition (keys up to and including four sharps and four flats)
- Transpose a melody up or down one octave
- Transpose a melody from one clef to another (Treble to Bass or Bass to Treble)
- Rewrite a melody at the same pitch in the alternate clef

Musical Terms and Signs
- Recognize, define or give the musical terms or signs as listed in the Basic Rudiments Workbook

Analysis
- Analyze a short musical composition, identifying any of the above theory requirements

Score:
  60 - 69 Pass; **70 - 79** Honors; **80 - 89** First Class Honors; **90 - 100** First Class Honors with Distinction

Ultimate Music Theory: *The Way to Score Success!*

UltimateMusicTheory.com © Copyright 2013 Gloryland Publishing. All Rights Reserved.

ULTIMATE MUSIC THEORY
BASIC EXAM SET #1 - EXAM #1

Total Score: ____ / 100

> ♪ **UMT Tip:** Before beginning your exam, write out the Circle of Fifths. Write the order of flats and sharps. Write the Major keys on the outside of the circle and the relative minor keys on the inside of the circle.

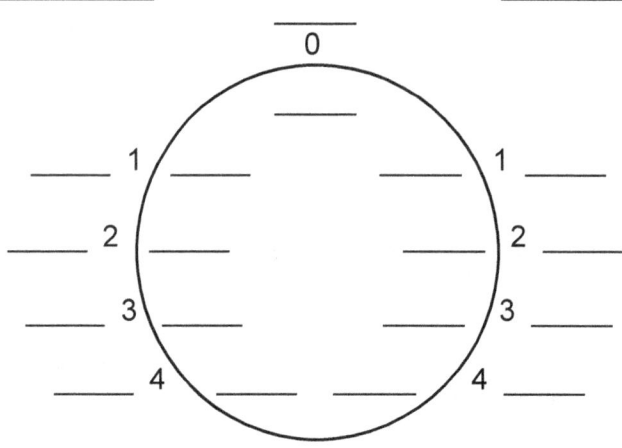

> ♪ **UMT Tip:** A Key Signature affects all the notes on the staff (and on ledger lines) with the same letter names.

1. a) Write the following notes in the Treble Clef. Use whole notes.

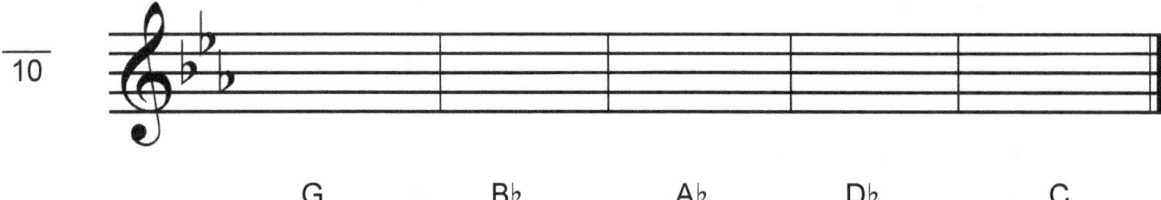

G   B♭   A♭   D♭   C

b) Name the following notes in the Bass Clef.

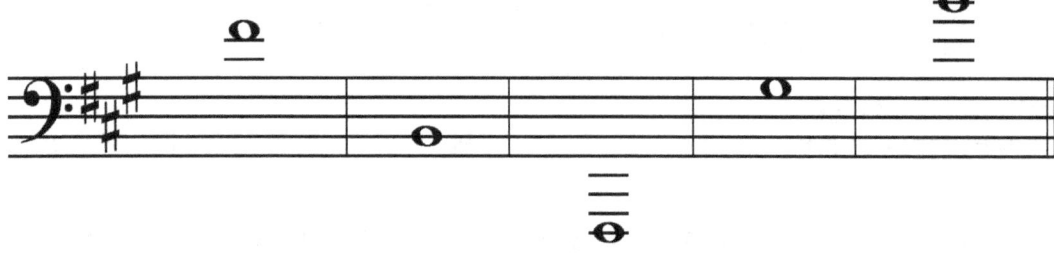

UltimateMusicTheory.com © Copyright 2013 Gloryland Publishing. All Rights Reserved.

ULTIMATE MUSIC THEORY
BASIC EXAM SET #1 - EXAM #1

♪ **UMT Tip:** The Dominant triad of a minor key contains the raised 7th (Leading note).

2. a) Write the following solid triads in root position in the Treble Clef. Use the correct Key Signature and any necessary accidentals. Use whole notes.

10

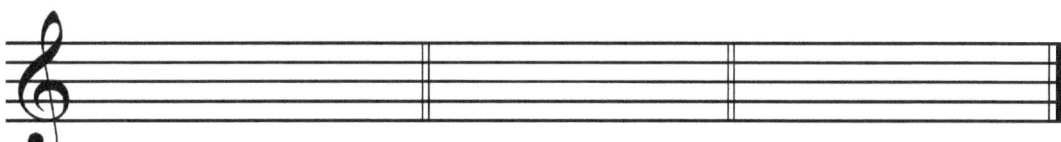

    Subdominant triad of   Dominant triad of   Tonic triad of
    A Major   b minor harmonic   E♭ Major

b) Write the following solid triads in root position in the Bass Clef. Use accidentals. Use whole notes.

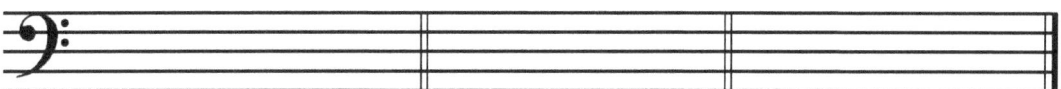

    Subdominant triad of   Dominant triad of   Tonic triad of
    B♭ Major   c minor harmonic   E Major

♪ **UMT Tip:** A Major triad consists of a Major 3rd and a Perfect 5th. A minor triad consists of a minor 3rd and a Perfect 5th.

c) Identify the following broken triads as Major or minor.

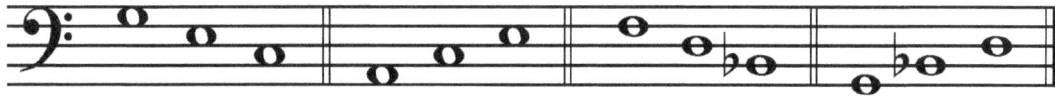

_____ _____ _____ _____

ULTIMATE MUSIC THEORY
BASIC EXAM SET #1 - EXAM #1

> ♪ **UMT Tip:** An interval is named based upon the Major Key of the lower (bottom) note.

3. Name each of the following intervals.

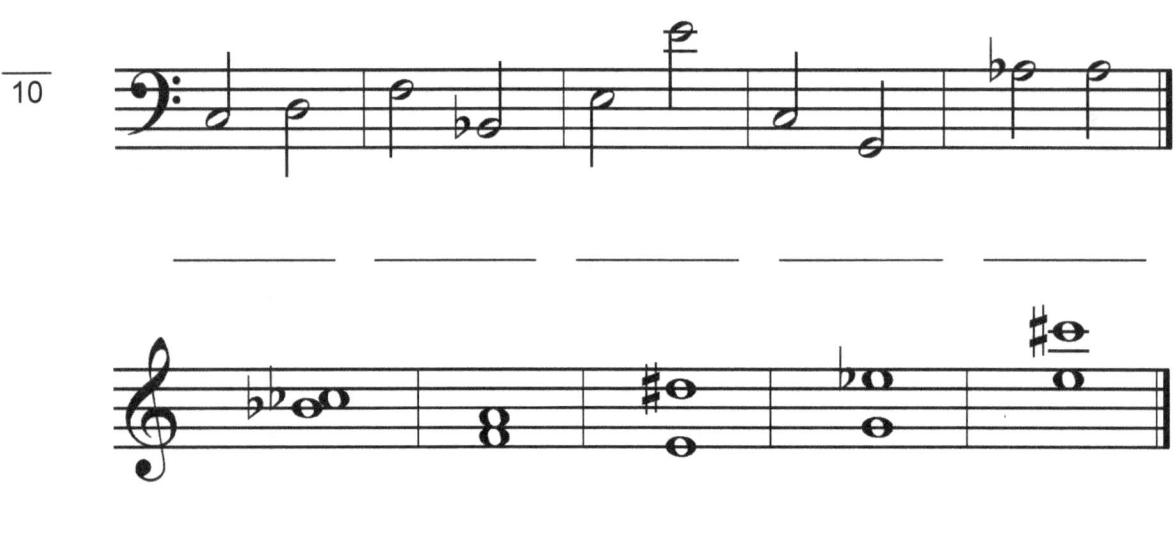

> ♪ **UMT Tip:** The Time Signature and Key Signature will remain the same as the original given melody. Rewrite the bar lines first before rewriting the notes.

4. Name the key of the following melody. Rewrite the melody at the same pitch in the Bass Clef.

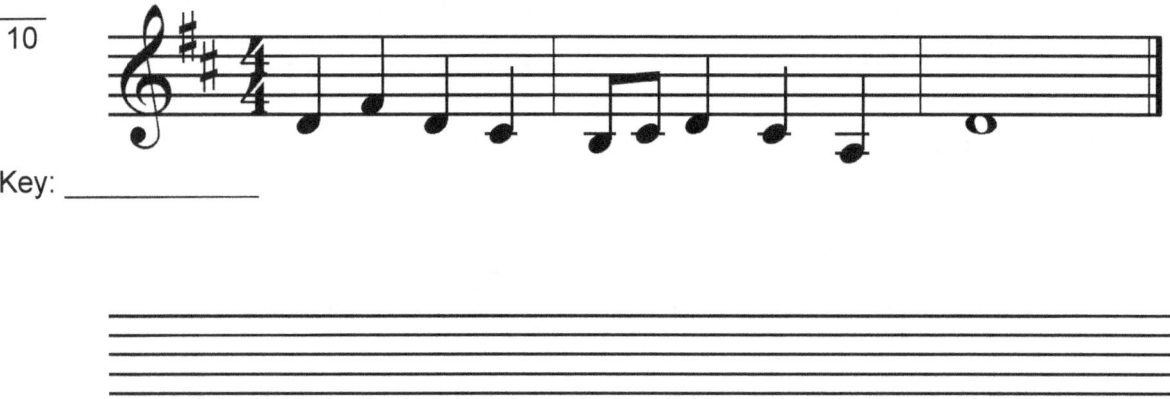

Key: _____

ULTIMATE MUSIC THEORY
BASIC EXAM SET #1 - EXAM #1

> ♪ **UMT Tip:** Scales may be written with or without a center bar line after the highest note. Either way is correct.

5. Write the following scales, ascending and descending, using the correct Key Signature and any necessary accidentals for each. Use whole notes.

___
10

a) C Major scale in the Treble Clef.

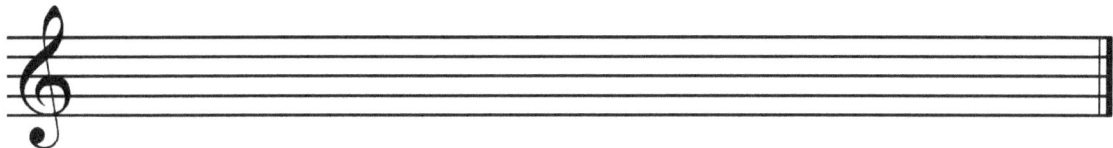

b) f minor melodic scale in the Bass Clef.

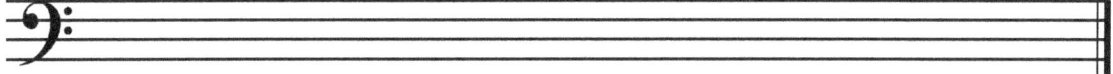

c) f sharp minor harmonic scale in the Bass Clef.

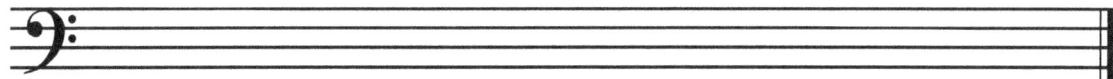

d) E Major scale in the Treble Clef.

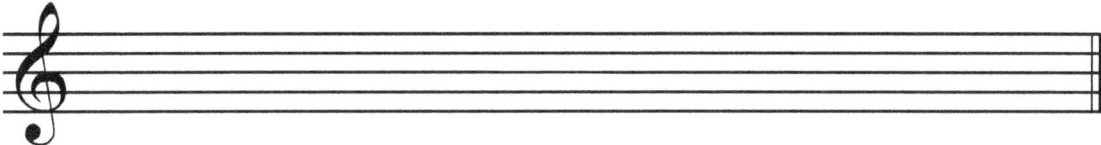

e) c minor scale, natural form, in the Treble Clef.

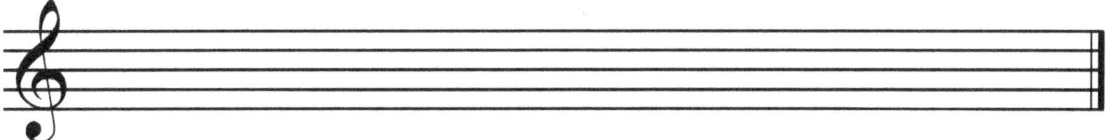

ULTIMATE MUSIC THEORY
BASIC EXAM SET #1 - EXAM #1

> ♪ **UMT Tip:** A diatonic semitone uses different letter names; a chromatic semitone uses the same letter name. An enharmonic equivalent is the same pitch using different letter names.

6. Name each of the following as: diatonic semitone or diatonic half step (**d.s.**)
    chromatic semitone or chromatic half step (**c.s.**)
    whole tone or whole step (**w.t.**)
    or enharmonic equivalent (**e.e.**)

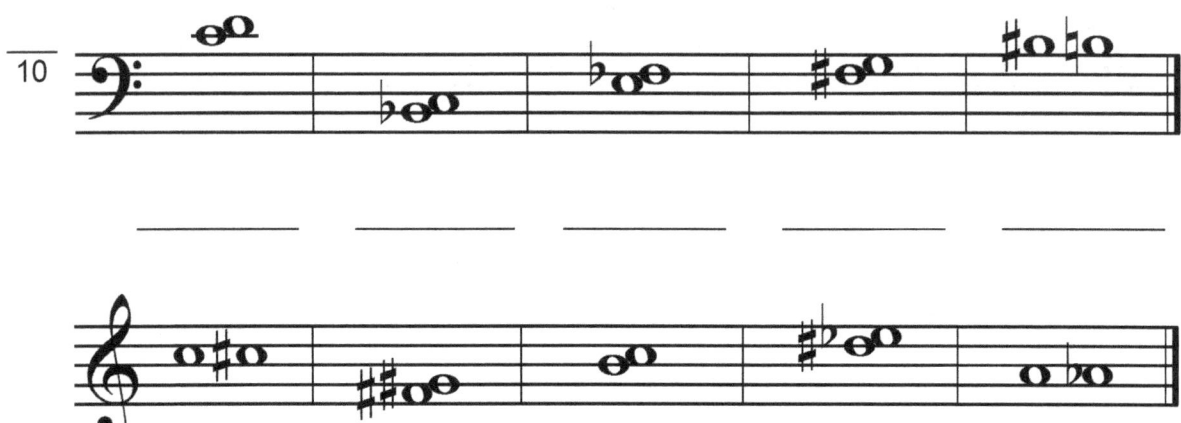

> ♪ **UMT Tip:** Use the Circle of Fifths to identify the Key Signatures.

7. a) Name the minor key for each of the following Key Signatures.
   b) Indicate whether the given note is the:
      Tonic note (**T**), Subdominant note (**SD**) or Dominant note (**D**).

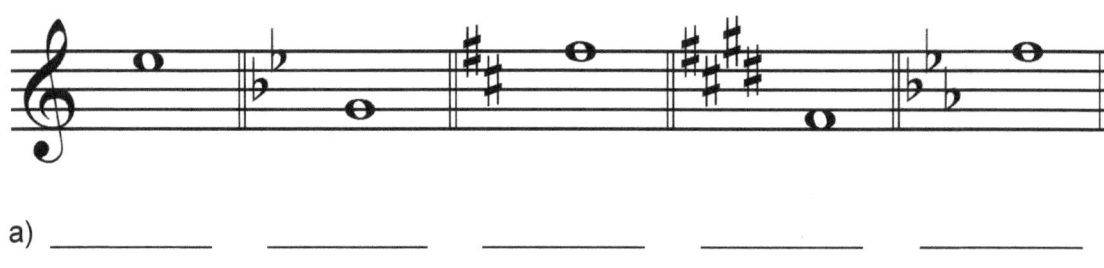

ULTIMATE MUSIC THEORY
BASIC EXAM SET #1 - EXAM #1

> ♪ **UMT Tip:** Bar lines are written from the top of the staff to the bottom of the staff.

8. a) Add bar lines to complete the following rhythms.

b) Add the Time Signature below the bracket for each of the following rhythms.

> ♪ **UMT Tip:** A breve rest (𝄺) is used for a whole measure of silence in $\frac{4}{2}$ time.
> A whole rest is used for a whole measure of silence in all other Time Signatures.

c) Add rests below each bracket to complete each measure.

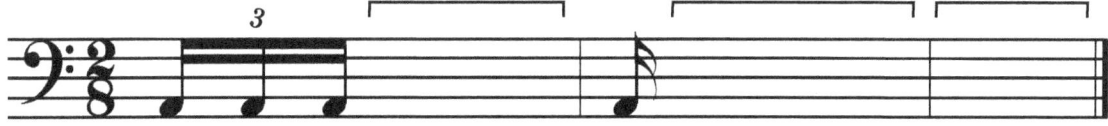

ULTIMATE MUSIC THEORY
BASIC EXAM SET #1 - EXAM #1

> ♪ **UMT Tip:** Match the terms that you know first. If you are not sure of a definition, leave it until you have finished, and then see what definitions are left.

9. Match each musical term with its English definition. (Not all definitions will be used.)

Term		Definition
dolce	_____	a) a little faster than *andante*
tempo	_____	b) very slow
andantino	_____	c) becoming softer
ritardando, rit.	_____	d) becoming louder
allegro	_____	e) repeat from the beginning
diminuendo, dim.	_____	f) sweet, gentle
largo	_____	g) at a moderate tempo
crescendo, cresc.	_____	h) speed at which music is performed
moderato	_____	i) repeat from the sign
da capo, D.C.	_____	j) slowing down gradually
		k) fast

ULTIMATE MUSIC THEORY
BASIC EXAM SET #1 - EXAM #1

> ♪ **UMT Tip:** When identifying the Key Signature, a minor key will usually have an accidental on the raised 7th note - the Leading note.

10. Analyze the following piece of music by answering the questions below.

Cloudy Saturday

Andante

S. McKibbon

a) Name the key of this piece. _____

b) Explain the tempo of this piece. _____

c) Add the Time Signature directly on the music.

d) Name the interval at the letter **A**. _____

e) Name the interval at the letter **B**. _____

f) Name the interval at the letter **C**. _____

g) Name the notes at the letters: D _____   E _____

h) Name the interval at the letter **F**. _____

i) Identify the triad at the letter **G** as Major or minor. _____

j) Identify the triad at the letter **G** as Solid or Broken. _____

UltimateMusicTheory.com © Copyright 2013 Gloryland Publishing. All Rights Reserved.

ULTIMATE MUSIC THEORY EXAM SERIES

_____   _____

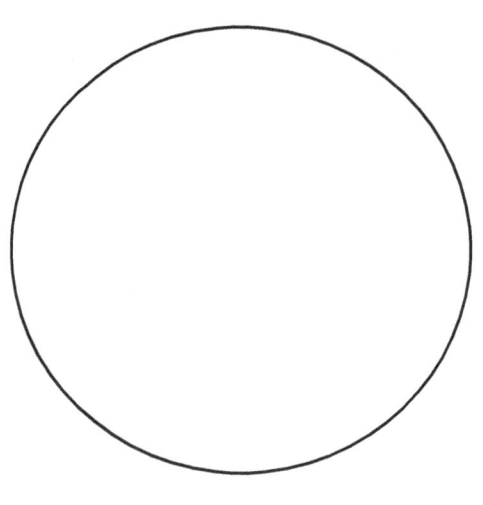

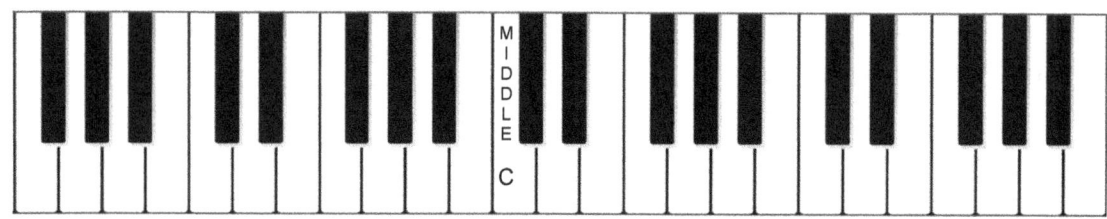

 UltimateMusicTheory.com © Copyright 2013 Gloryland Publishing. All Rights Reserved.

ULTIMATE MUSIC THEORY EXAM SERIES

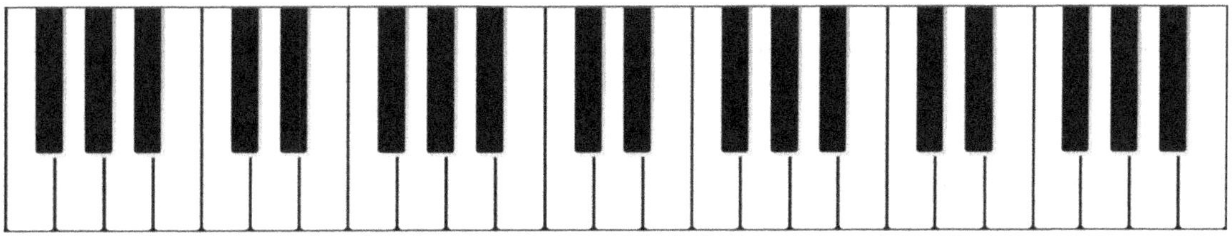

UltimateMusicTheory.com © Copyright 2013 Gloryland Publishing. All Rights Reserved.

ULTIMATE MUSIC THEORY
BASIC EXAM SET #1 - EXAM #2

Total Score: ____ / 100

> ♪ **UMT Tip:** Before beginning your exam, write the Circle of Fifths. Write the order of flats and sharps. Write the Major keys on the outside of the circle and the relative minor keys on the inside of the circle.

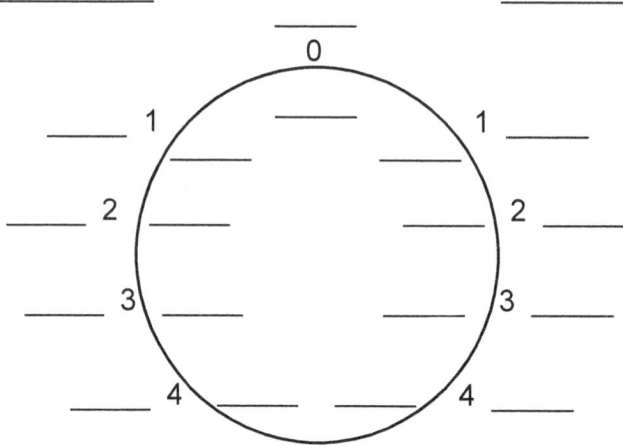

> ♪ **UMT Tip:** When writing a dotted half note, the dot goes in the space beside the note for a space note, and in the space above the note for a line note.

1. a) Write the following notes in the Bass Clef. Use dotted half notes.

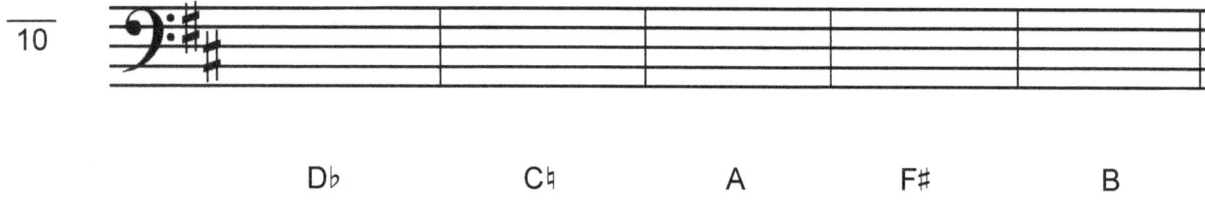

Db C♮ A F# B

b) Name the following notes in the Treble Clef.

UltimateMusicTheory.com © Copyright 2013 Gloryland Publishing. All Rights Reserved.

ULTIMATE MUSIC THEORY
BASIC EXAM SET #1 - EXAM #2

> ♪ **UMT Tip:** The root note is the bottom (lower) note of the triad.

2. a) Name the Major key for each Key Signature.
   b) Name the root note of each triad.

a) Major key: _____   _____   _____

b) Root note: _____   _____   _____

a) Major key: _____   _____   _____

b) Root note: _____   _____   _____

> ♪ **UMT Tip:** A Major triad has an interval of a Major 3 and a Perfect 5 above the root.
> A minor triad has an interval of a minor 3 and a Perfect 5 above the root.

c) Identify the following triads as Major or minor.

_____   _____   _____   _____

ULTIMATE MUSIC THEORY
BASIC EXAM SET #1 - EXAM #2

> ♪ **UMT Tip:** When writing a harmonic interval, and there is no room for correct placement of accidentals, it is acceptable to place the accidental further away from the upper note.

3. a) Write the following harmonic intervals above each of the given notes. Use whole notes.

      minor 3   Perfect 1   Perfect 8   Major 7   Perfect 4

b) Write the following melodic intervals above each of the given notes. Use half notes.

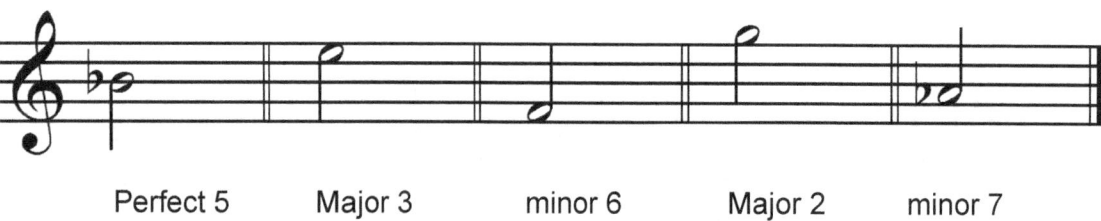

      Perfect 5   Major 3   minor 6   Major 2   minor 7

> ♪ **UMT Tip:** Rewrite the bar lines first before rewriting the notes.

4. Name the key of the following melody. Transpose it down one octave into the Bass Clef. Use the correct Key Signature.

Key: _____

ULTIMATE MUSIC THEORY
BASIC EXAM SET #1 - EXAM #2

> ♪ **UMT Tip:** Scales may be written with or without a center bar line after the highest note. Either way is correct.

5. Write the following scales, ascending and descending, using accidentals instead of a Key Signature. Use whole notes.

__
10   a) f sharp minor, melodic form, in the Treble Clef.

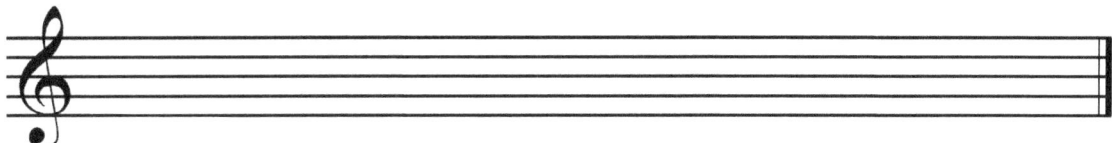

b) F Major in the Bass Clef.

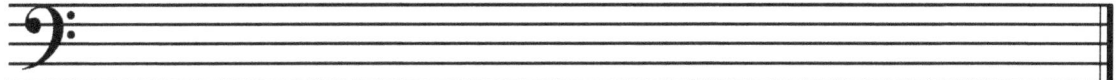

c) B flat Major in the Treble Clef.

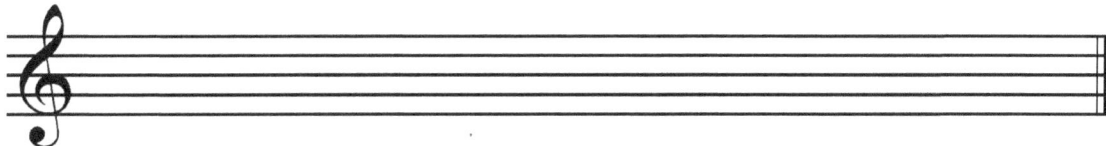

d) c sharp minor, natural form, in the Bass Clef.

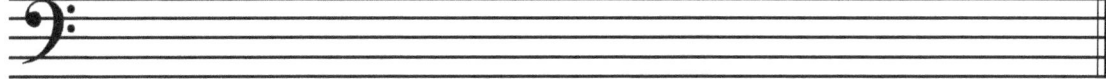

e) g minor, harmonic form, in the Treble Clef.

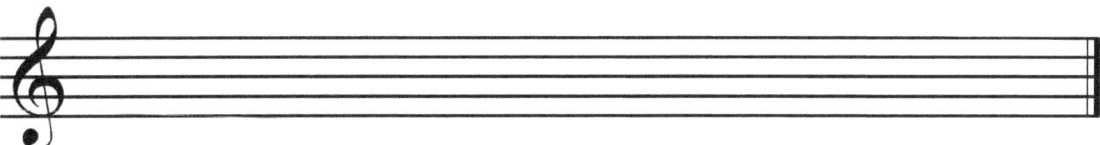

UltimateMusicTheory.com © Copyright 2013 Gloryland Publishing. All Rights Reserved.

ULTIMATE MUSIC THEORY
BASIC EXAM SET #1 - EXAM #2

> ♪ **UMT Tip:** An enharmonic equivalent is the same pitch using different letter names.

6. Name each of the following notes. On the staff below, write the enharmonic equivalent of each note. Use whole notes. Name each of the notes that you have written.

> ♪ **UMT Tip:** Use the Circle of Fifths to identify the Key Signatures.

7. a) Name the minor key for each of the following Key Signatures.
   b) Indicate whether the given note is the:
       Tonic note (**T**),   Subdominant note (**SD**)   or   Dominant note (**D**).

a) _____ _____ _____ _____ _____

b) _____ _____ _____ _____ _____

ULTIMATE MUSIC THEORY
BASIC EXAM SET #1 - EXAM #2

> ♪ **UMT Tip:** Scoop each Basic Beat.

8. a) Add bar lines to complete the following rhythms.

> ♪ **UMT Tip:** When adding Time Signatures, look for an anacrusis (incomplete measure).

b) Add the Time Signature below the bracket for each of the following rhythms.

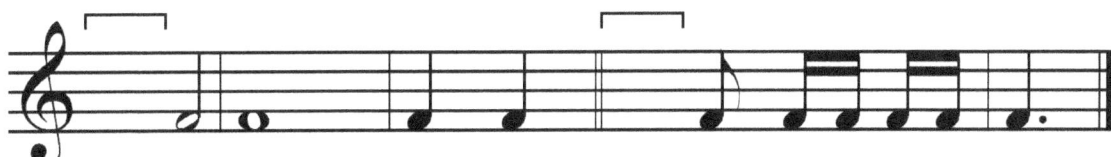

c) Add rests below each bracket to complete each measure.

ULTIMATE MUSIC THEORY
BASIC EXAM SET #1 - EXAM #2

> ♪ **UMT Tip:** As you match each term with the correct definition, draw a line through the letter beside the definition to show that you have used that definition.

9. Match each musical term with its English definition. (Not all definitions will be used.)

__10__

Term		Definition
dal segno, D.S.	_____	a) slow
a tempo	_____	b) detached
grazioso	_____	c) return to the original tempo
lento	_____	d) fairly fast (a little slower than *allegro*)
marcato, marc.	_____	e) held, sustained
staccato	_____	f) becoming softer
allegretto	_____	g) graceful
presto	_____	h) repeat from the sign
tenuto	_____	i) marked or stressed
decrescendo, decresc.	_____	j) smooth
		k) very fast

ULTIMATE MUSIC THEORY
BASIC EXAM SET #1 - EXAM #2

> ♪ **UMT Tip:** The first measure of a piece of music is the first full measure. An anacrusis (upbeat) is part of the final measure of the piece. It is not counted as measure 1.

10. Analyze the following piece of music by answering the questions below.

Peanut Butter

Moderato   S. McKibbon

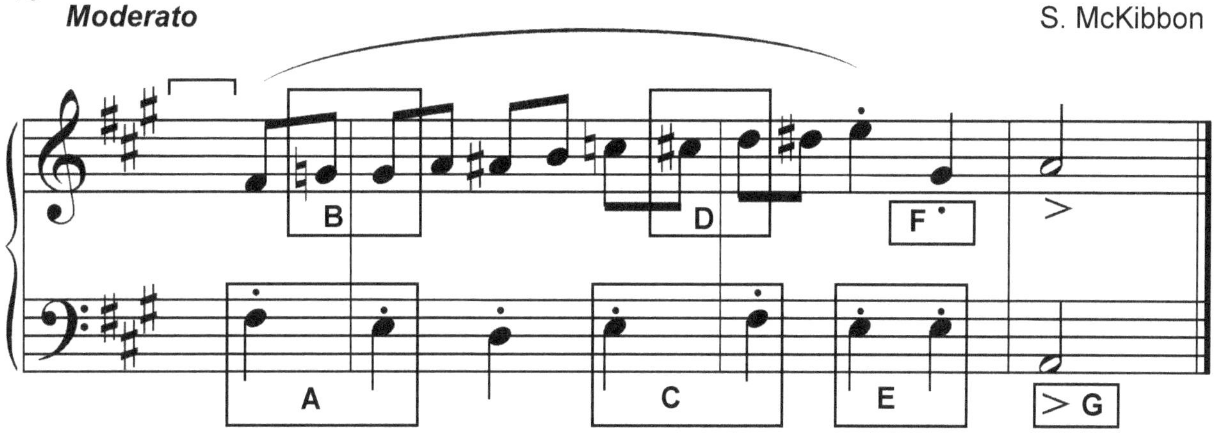

a) Name the title of this piece. _____

b) Explain the tempo of this piece. _____

c) Add the Time Signature directly on the music.

d) Name the intervals at the following letters as:
   d.s. (diatonic semitone),   **c.s.** (chromatic semitone)   or   **w.t.** (whole tone).

   A _____   B _____   C _____   D _____

e) Name the interval at the letter **E**. _____

f) Explain the sign at the letter **F**. _____

g) Explain the sign at the letter **G**. _____

h) How many measures are in this piece? _____

i) What count does this piece of music begin on? _____

UltimateMusicTheory.com © Copyright 2013 Gloryland Publishing. All Rights Reserved.

ULTIMATE MUSIC THEORY EXAM SERIES

_____   _____

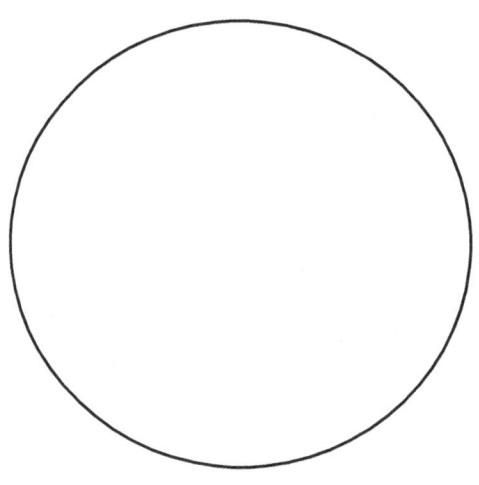

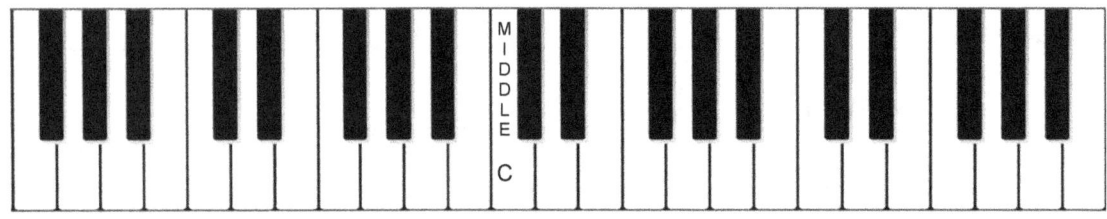

UltimateMusicTheory.com © Copyright 2013 Gloryland Publishing. All Rights Reserved.

ULTIMATE MUSIC THEORY EXAM SERIES

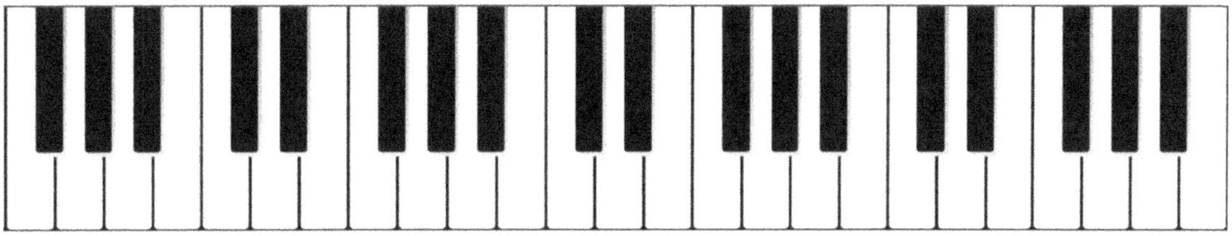

UltimateMusicTheory.com © Copyright 2013 Gloryland Publishing. All Rights Reserved.

ULTIMATE MUSIC THEORY
BASIC EXAM SET #1 - EXAM #3

Total Score: ___ / 100

1. a) Write the following notes on ledger lines either above or below the Treble Clef. Use quarter notes.

/10

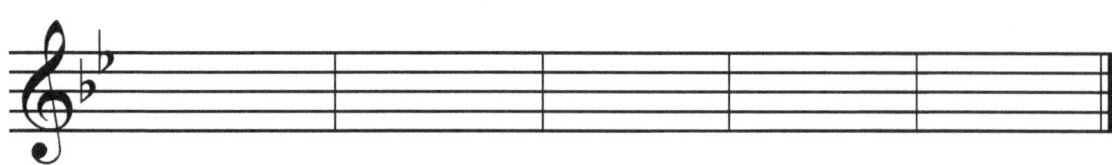

    Ab   E♮   C   G#   Bb

    b) Name the note below each bracket.

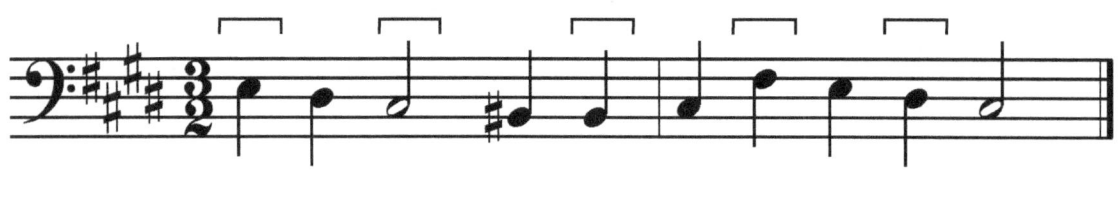

2. a) Write the following solid triads in root position in the Bass Clef. Use the correct Key Signature and any necessary accidentals. Use whole notes.

/10

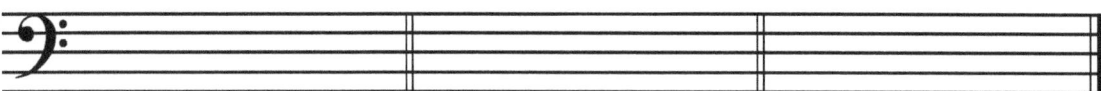

    Tonic triad of   Subdominant triad of   Dominant triad of
    A Major   f minor harmonic   b minor harmonic

    b) Identify the root of the following triads as the Tonic, Subdominant or Dominant note.

    C Major   D Major   e minor   d minor

UltimateMusicTheory.com © Copyright 2013 Gloryland Publishing. All Rights Reserved.

ULTIMATE MUSIC THEORY
BASIC EXAM SET #1 - EXAM #3

3. a) Name the following melodic intervals.

_____   _____   _____   _____   _____

b) Write the following harmonic intervals above each of the given notes. Use whole notes.

Perfect 4   minor 2   Major 3   Major 7   Perfect 5

4. Name the key of the following melody. Transpose it up one octave into the Treble Clef. Use the correct Key Signature.

Key: _____

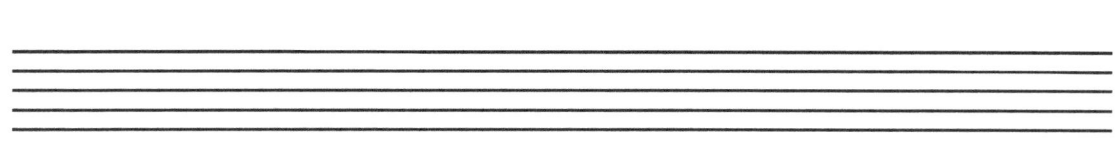

ULTIMATE MUSIC THEORY
BASIC EXAM SET #1 - EXAM #3

5. Write the following scales, ascending and descending, using a Key Signature and any necessary accidentals. Use whole notes.

$\overline{10}$

a) e minor, harmonic form, in the Bass Clef.

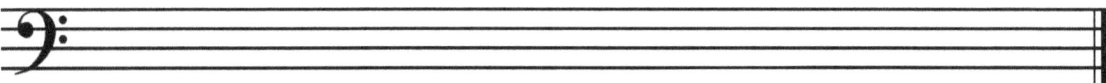

b) A Major in the Bass Clef.

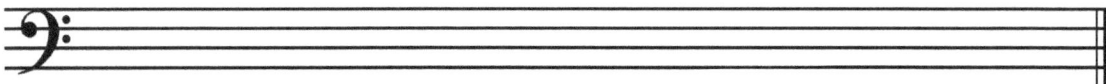

c) b minor, melodic form, in the Treble Clef.

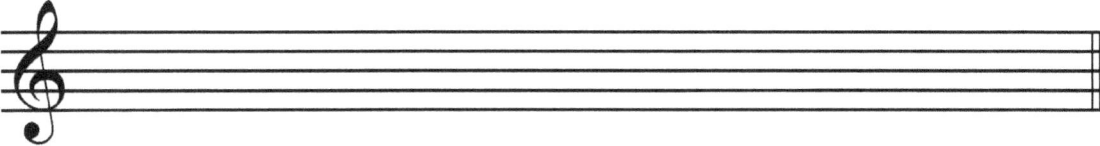

d) a minor, natural form, in the Bass Clef.

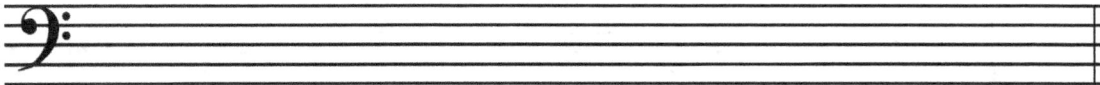

e) E flat Major in the Treble Clef.

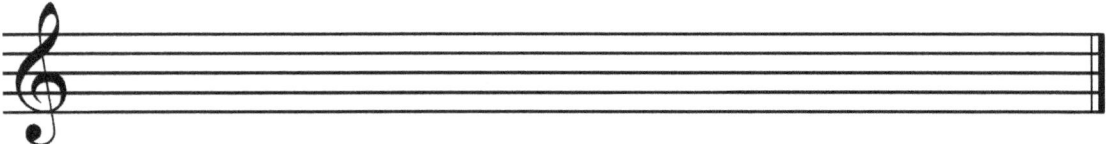

UltimateMusicTheory.com © Copyright 2013 Gloryland Publishing. All Rights Reserved.

ULTIMATE MUSIC THEORY
BASIC EXAM SET #1 - EXAM #3

6. a) Write the note that is a whole tone (whole step) above each of the following notes. Use whole notes.

b) Write the note that is a diatonic semitone (diatonic half step) below each of the following notes. Use whole notes.

7. Add rests below each bracket to complete each measure.

ULTIMATE MUSIC THEORY
BASIC EXAM SET #1 - EXAM #3

8. a) Add bar lines to complete the following rhythms.

b) Add the correct Time Signature below each bracket to complete the following rhythms.

ULTIMATE MUSIC THEORY
BASIC EXAM SET #1 - EXAM #3

9. Match each musical sign with its English definition. (Not all definitions will be used.)

Sign   **Definition**

♩ ♩ _____   a) play one octave below the written pitch

8va‾‾‾¬ _____   b) play the notes legato (smooth)

8va‾‾‾⌋ _____   c) from the sign

𝄐 _____   d) hold for the combined value of the tied notes

𝄋 _____   e) a stressed note

♩ ♩ ♩ _____   f) play one octave above the written pitch

Ped. _____   g) repeat the music within the double bar lines

♩̌ _____   h) pause; hold the note or rest longer than its written value

𝄎 _____   i) from the beginning

♩. _____   j) pedal marking

                        k) detached

ULTIMATE MUSIC THEORY
BASIC EXAM SET #1 - EXAM #3

10. Analyze the following musical excerpt by answering the questions below.

__10__

Allegro Moderato

W. A. Mozart

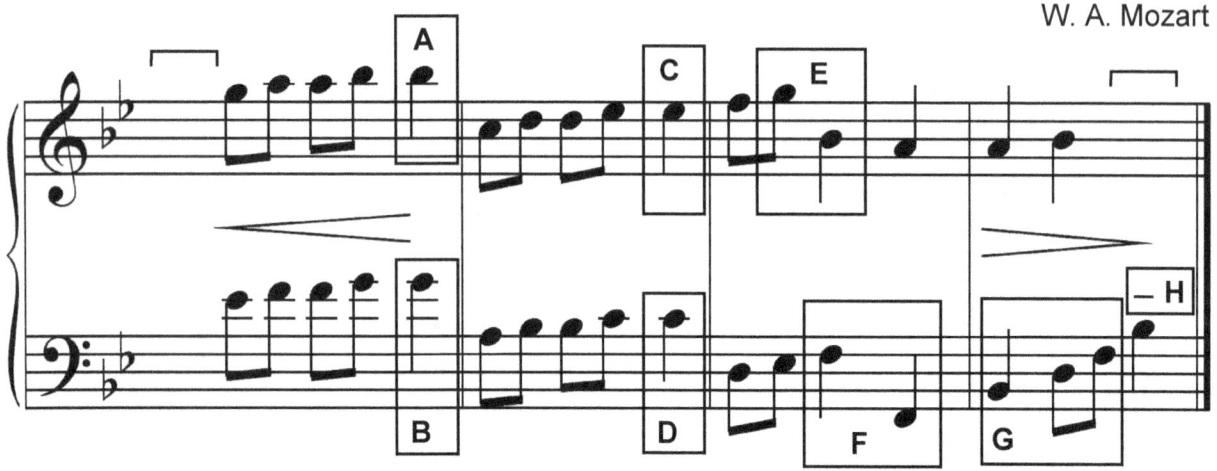

a) Name the composer of this excerpt. _____

b) Name the key of this piece. _____

c) Add the Time Signature directly on the music.

d) Explain the dynamic in measure 1. _____

e) Name the notes at the letters: A _____ B _____

f) Name the notes at the letters: C _____ D _____

g) Name the intervals at the letters: E _____ F _____

h) Is the triad at the letter **G** Solid or Broken? _____

i) Add the missing rest(s) under the bracket in measure 4.

j) Explain the sign at the letter **H**. _____

UltimateMusicTheory.com © Copyright 2013 Gloryland Publishing. All Rights Reserved.

ULTIMATE MUSIC THEORY EXAM SERIES

_____   _____

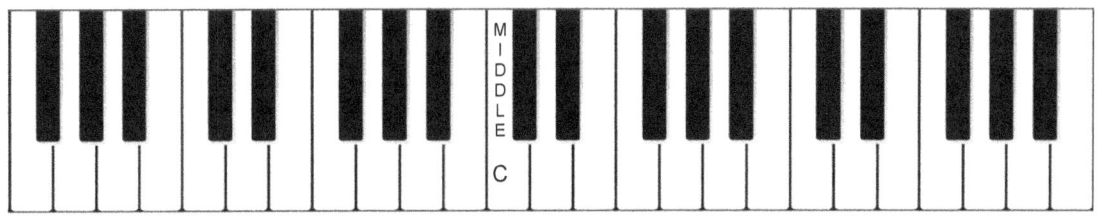

UltimateMusicTheory.com © Copyright 2013 Gloryland Publishing. All Rights Reserved.

ULTIMATE MUSIC THEORY EXAM SERIES

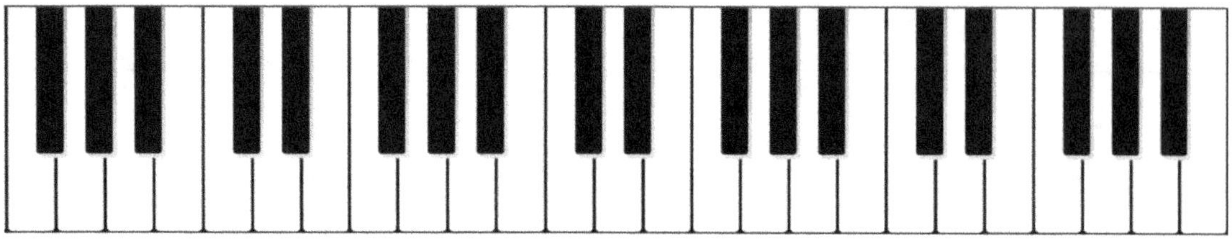

UltimateMusicTheory.com © Copyright 2013 Gloryland Publishing. All Rights Reserved.

ULTIMATE MUSIC THEORY
BASIC EXAM SET #1 - EXAM #4

Total Score: ___ / 100

1. a) Write the following notes on ledger lines either above or below the Treble Clef. Use half notes.

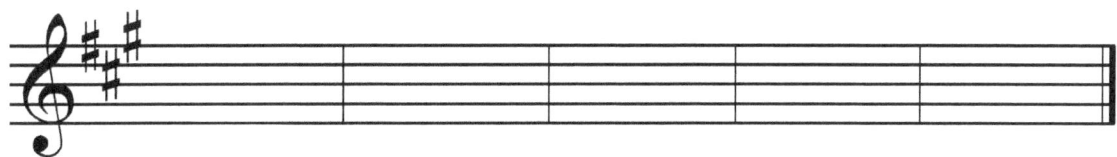

    A   G♭   C♯   F♯   E♭

b) Name the note below each bracket.

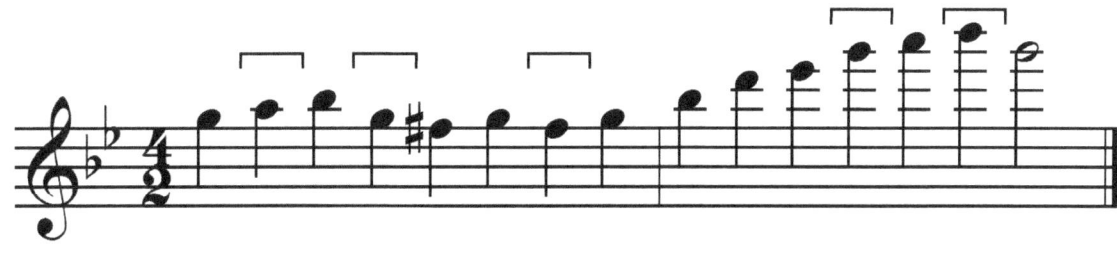

c) Write the following notes in the Bass Clef. Use whole notes.

    A♭   G♭   B♮   E♯   D♭

d) Name the note below each bracket.

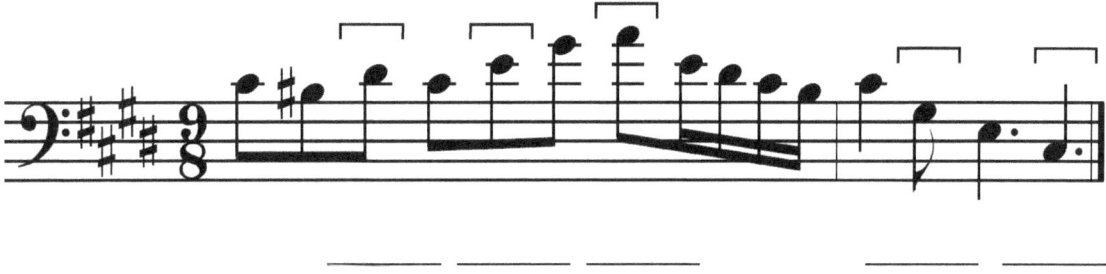

UltimateMusicTheory.com © Copyright 2013 Gloryland Publishing. All Rights Reserved.

ULTIMATE MUSIC THEORY
BASIC EXAM SET #1 - EXAM #4

2. a) Write the following solid triads in root position in the Treble Clef. Use the correct Key Signature and any necessary accidentals. Use whole notes.

___
10

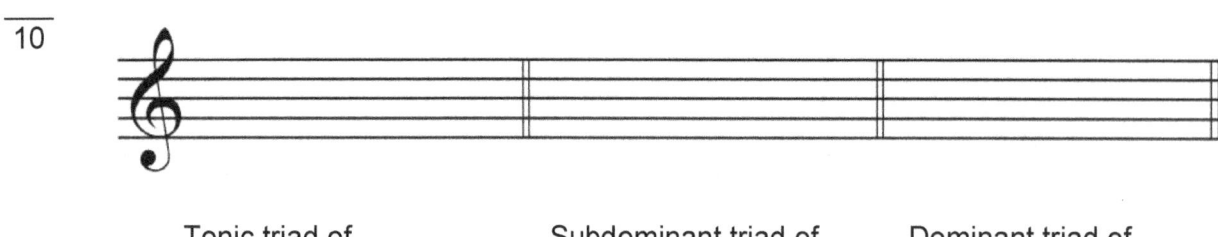

      Tonic triad of   Subdominant triad of   Dominant triad of
      A Major   f minor harmonic   b minor harmonic

b) Match each description in the left column with the correct triad in the right column.

Description	Answer		Triad
Dominant triad of G Major	f	a)	
Tonic triad of d minor harmonic	___	b)	
Subdominant triad of g minor harmonic	___	c)	
Dominant triad of b minor harmonic	___	d)	
Tonic triad of E Major	___	e)	
Subdominant triad of C Major	___	f)	
Dominant triad of c sharp minor harmonic	___	g)	
Tonic triad of A flat Major	___	h)	

ULTIMATE MUSIC THEORY
BASIC EXAM SET #1 - EXAM #4

3. a) Name the intervals below the brackets.

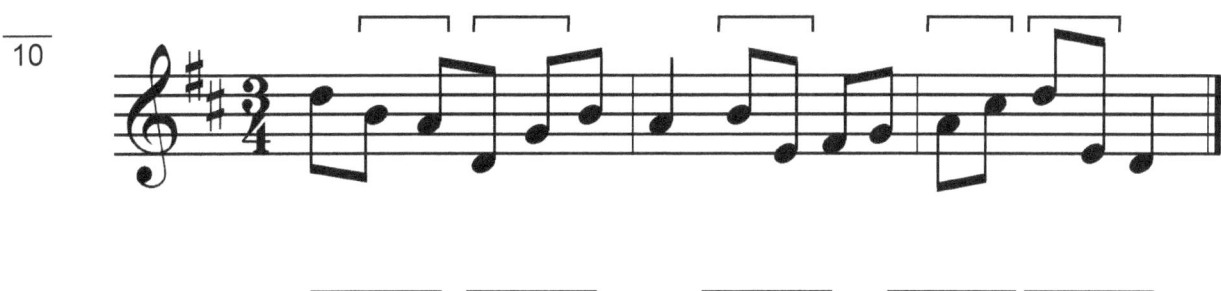

b) Write the following harmonic intervals above each of the given notes. Use whole notes.

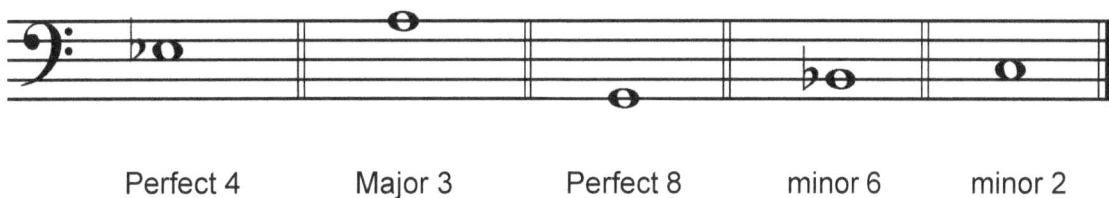

Perfect 4   Major 3   Perfect 8   minor 6   minor 2

4. Name the key of the following melody. Transpose it down one octave in the Bass Clef. Use the correct Key Signature.

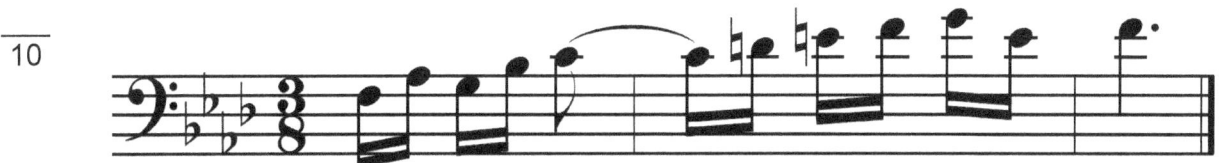

Key: _____

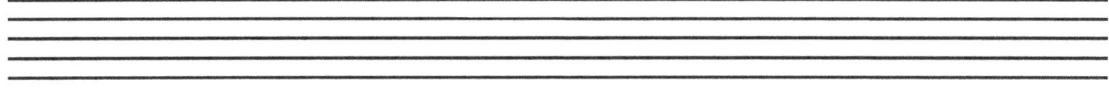

ULTIMATE MUSIC THEORY
BASIC EXAM SET #1 - EXAM #4

5. Add the correct Key Signature and any necessary accidentals to form the following scales.

__10__

a) d minor, harmonic form, in the Treble Clef.

b) b minor, natural form, in the Bass Clef.

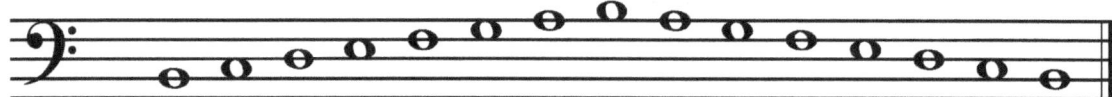

c) G Major, in the Treble Clef.

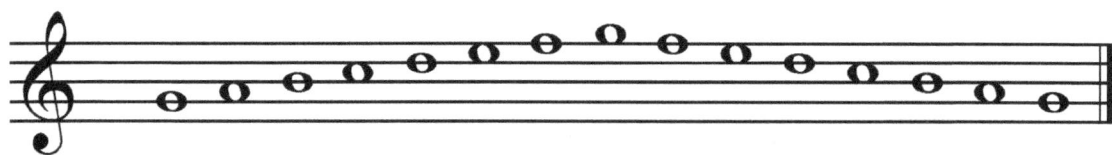

d) c minor, melodic form, in the Bass Clef.

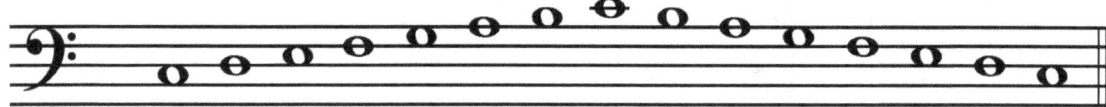

e) c sharp minor, harmonic form, in the Treble Clef.

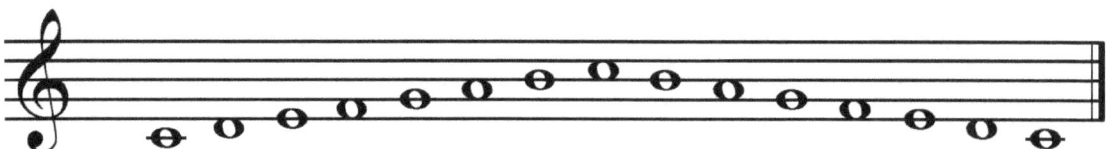

UltimateMusicTheory.com © Copyright 2013 Gloryland Publishing. All Rights Reserved.

ULTIMATE MUSIC THEORY
BASIC EXAM SET #1 - EXAM #4

6. Name each of the following as: **d.s.** (diatonic semitone), **c.s.** (chromatic semitone)
   w.t. (whole tone)   or **e.e.** (enharmonic equivalent)

7. Add bar lines to complete the following rhythms.

ULTIMATE MUSIC THEORY
BASIC EXAM SET #1 - EXAM #4

8. Add rests below each bracket to complete each measure.

ULTIMATE MUSIC THEORY
BASIC EXAM SET #1 - EXAM #4

9. Match each musical term with its English definition. (Not all definitions will be used.)

Term		Definition
fortissimo, *ff*	____	a) soft
mano sinistra, M.S.	____	b) moderately soft
piano, *p*	____	c) very soft
Tempo primo (Tempo I)	____	d) loud
mezzo piano, *mp*	____	e) moderately loud
forte, *f*	____	f) very loud
pianissimo, *pp*	____	g) left hand
mezzo forte, *mf*	____	h) return to the original tempo
mano destra, M.D.	____	i) right hand
D.C. al fine	____	j) moderately slow, at a walking pace
		k) repeat from the beginning and end at *Fine*

___/10

ULTIMATE MUSIC THEORY
BASIC EXAM SET #1 - EXAM #4

10. Analyze the following excerpt by answering the questions below.

Minuet in F

W. A. Mozart

a) Add the Time Signature directly on the music.

b) Name the key of this piece. _____

c) Explain the sign at the letter **A**. _____

d) Explain the sign at the letter **B**. _____

e) Name the intervals at the letters: C _____   D _____

f) Explain the sign at the letter **E**. _____

g) Explain the sign at the letter **F**. _____

h) Explain the sign at the letter **G**. _____

i) The note at the letter **H** is the: ☐ Tonic   ☐ Subdominant   ☐ Dominant

j) The note at the letter **I** is the: ☐ Tonic   ☐ Subdominant   ☐ Dominant

UltimateMusicTheory.com © Copyright 2013 Gloryland Publishing. All Rights Reserved.

ULTIMATE MUSIC THEORY EXAM SERIES

_____   _____

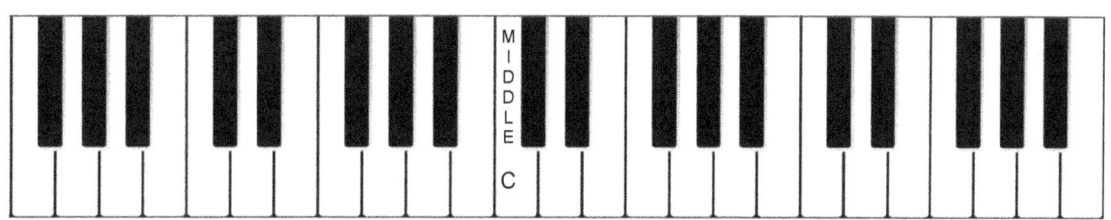

UltimateMusicTheory.com © Copyright 2013 Gloryland Publishing. All Rights Reserved.

ULTIMATE MUSIC THEORY EXAM SERIES

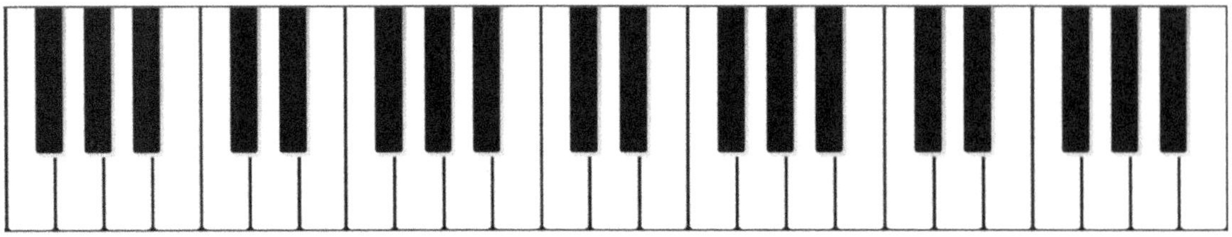

UltimateMusicTheory.com © Copyright 2013 Gloryland Publishing. All Rights Reserved.

ULTIMATE MUSIC THEORY EXAM SERIES

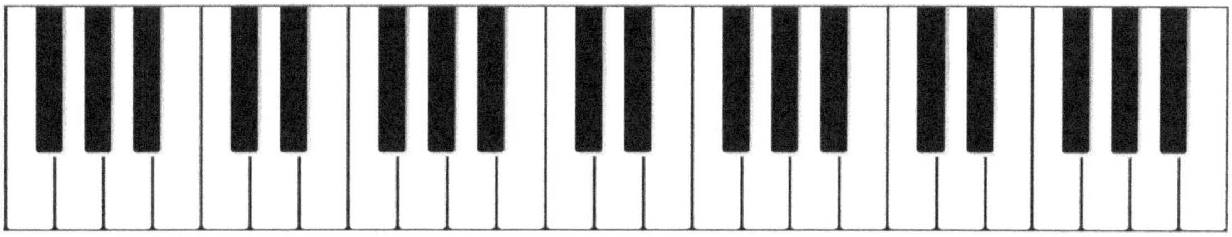

UltimateMusicTheory.com © Copyright 2013 Gloryland Publishing. All Rights Reserved.

Workbooks, Exams, Answers, Online Courses, App & More!

A Proven Step-by-Step System to Learn Theory Faster - from Beginner to Advanced.

Innovative techniques designed to develop a complete understanding of music theory, to enhance sight reading, ear training, creativity, composition and musical expression.

All UMT Series have matching Answer Books!

The UMT Rudiments Series - Beginner A, Beginner B, Beginner C, Prep 1, Prep 2, Basic, Intermediate, Advanced & Complete (All-In-One)

♪ 12 Lessons, Review Tests, and a Final Exam to develop confidence
♪ Music Theory Guide & Chart for fast and easy reference of theory concepts
♪ 80 Flashcards for fun drills to dramatically increase retention & comprehension

Rudiments Exam Series - Preparatory, Basic, Intermediate & Advanced

♪ 8 Exams plus UMT Tips on How to Score 100% on Theory Exams

Each Rudiments Workbook correlates to a Supplemental Workbook.

The UMT Supplemental Series - Prep Level, Level 1, Level 2, Level 3, Level 4, Level 5, Level 6, Level 7, Level 8 & Complete (All-In-One) Level

♪ Form & Analysis and Music History - Composers, Eras & Musical Styles
♪ Melody Writing using ICE - Imagine, Compose & Explore
♪ 12 Lessons, Review Tests, Final Exam and 80 Flashcards for quick study

Supplemental Exam Series - Level 5, Level 6, Level 7 & Level 8

♪ 8 Exams to successfully prepare for nationally recognized Theory Exams

UMT Online Courses, Music Theory App & More

♪ UMT Certification Course, Teachers Membership & Elite Educator Program
♪ Ultimate Music Theory App correlates to the Rudiments Workbooks
♪ Free Resources - Teachers Guide, Music Theory Blogs, videos & downloads

Go To: **UltimateMusicTheory.com**

www.ingramcontent.com/pod-product-compliance
Lightning Source LLC
Chambersburg PA
CBHW081735100526
44591CB00016B/2621